Tommy Prince

Terry Barber

FIRST
NATIONS
SERIES

Tommy Prince is published by
Grass Roots Press, a division of Literacy Services of Canada Ltd.

www.grassrootsbooks.net

ACKNOWLEDGEMENTS

We acknowledge the financial support of the Government of Canada through the Canada Book Fund (CBF) for our publishing activities.

Produced with the assistance of
the Government of Alberta, Alberta
Multimedia Development Fund.

Alberta
Government

Editor: Dr. Pat Campbell
Image research: Dr. Pat Campbell
Book design: Lara Minja, Lime Design Inc.

Library and Archives Canada Cataloguing in Publication

Barber, Terry, date, author
        Tommy Prince / Terry Barber.

(First Nations)
ISBN 978–1–77153–043–9 (pbk.)

        1. Prince, Tommy. 2. Soldiers—Canada—Biography. 3. Ojibwa Indians—Canada—Biography. 4. Readers for new literates. I. Title. II. Series: Barber, Terry, date. First Nations.

PE1126.N43B36785 2015   428.6'2   C2015-902587-7

Printed in Canada.

Contents

Like Tommy, this soldier gets ready to jump.

The First Jump

The airplane flies high above the earth.
Tommy stands by the airplane door.
The door is open. Tommy's stomach is
in a knot. He is afraid. Tommy jumps
from the airplanc.

The soldier's parachute opens.

The First Jump

Tommy's parachute opens. He feels the wind on his face. Tommy's feet hit the ground. His first jump from an airplane goes well.

Tommy is a soldier. Tommy loves his country. He wants to help win the war.

Tommy becomes one of Canada's best soldiers.

Like this family, Tommy lives in a tent.

Early Years

Tommy Prince is born in a tent in 1915. Tommy is the great-great-grandson of Chief Peguis. In the early 1800s, Chief Peguis helps the white settlers. He helps prevent the settlers from starving. Like Chief Peguis, Tommy is born to lead.

Chief Peguis is born in 1774 and dies in 1864.

Two Ojibway hunters in the woods.

Early Years

Tommy's family lives on the Brokenhead **Reserve**. Tommy has ten brothers and sisters. Tommy's father teaches him to hunt and trap animals. Tommy learns to be silent in the woods.

Brokenhead Reserve is part of the Ojibway Nation.

A hunter carries fresh meat from the woods.

Early Years

Tommy hunts all the time. Tommy knows he must be silent. Tommy knows he might get only one shot at an animal. He learns to shoot a gun with skill. When Tommy goes into the woods, he comes back with fresh meat.

Tommy joins the Army Cadets.

A World War II poster.

Tommy Joins the Army

Tommy joins the Army. Tommy is 24 years old. He wants to fight for his country. Tommy spends two years in training with the RCE. This unit builds bridges and fixes roads. Tommy does not see action for two years.

RCE stands for Royal Canadian Engineers.

Paratroopers train from a tower.

Tommy Joins the Army

Tommy wants to become a **paratrooper**. In 1942, he goes to parachute school. The training is hard. Tommy passes the tests. Tommy is a good paratrooper. He jumps, lands, and then hides quickly. Soon, the Army promotes Tommy to Sergeant.

Soldiers from the Devil's Brigade.

The Devil's Brigade

The Army sees that Tommy has many skills. The Army asks Tommy to join a special unit. Tommy joins the Devil's Brigade. These men carry out secret **missions**. These men know how to fight. These men know how to live off the land.

The Devil's Brigade includes Canadian and American soldiers.

Devil's Brigade soldiers learn
how to use machine guns.

The Devil's Brigade

The men of the Devil's Brigade train hard. They learn hand-to-hand **combat**. They learn how to use all kinds of weapons. They learn how to climb mountains. They learn how to spy. The Devil's Brigade goes to Italy in 1944.

A farmhouse in Italy, 1944.

The Devil's Brigade

Tommy's job is to spy on the Germans. One night, Tommy enters an empty farmhouse. He sets up a phone line. Tommy spends three days in the farmhouse. He phones his unit. Tommy reports on the Germans.

The farmhouse is only 600 feet from the German camp.

A gun fight cuts the phone wire.

The Devil's Brigade

On the third day, the phone line stops working. Tommy has a plan. He pretends to be a farmer. He walks outside. The Germans can see Tommy. He bends down as if to tie his shoelace. Instead, he fixes the phone line.

Tommy wins the Military Medal for bravery.

Like Tommy, these men prepare for night duty.

The Devil's Brigade

Tommy spies behind German lines
many times. Tommy likes to go alone.
Tommy says the white men of the
Devil's Brigade make too much noise.
Tommy wears moccasins. He goes
behind German lines like a ghost in
the night.

Captured German soldiers walk to a prison camp.

The Devil's Brigade

Later in 1944, the Devil's Brigade goes to France. Tommy looks for an enemy camp. He is alone. He walks 72 hours without food, water, or sleep. Then he sees the German camp. Tommy returns with his unit. Tommy and his unit capture 1,000 German soldiers.

Tommy (on right) and his brother, 1945.

Tommy Returns Home

Tommy returns to Canada in 1945. Tommy is one of Canada's most decorated soldiers. Tommy receives eight medals. As a soldier, Tommy is the bravest of the brave. But Tommy's biggest battle is still ahead of him.

World War II ends on September 2, 1945.

This soldier can vote because he is white.

Tommy Returns Home

Tommy and other **Indian** soldiers are willing to die for Canada. But when the war ends, they are not treated like heroes. White soldiers are the heroes. Tommy does not get the same benefits as white **veterans.** Indian veterans are treated like second-class citizens.

Indians cannot vote in federal elections.

Tommy serves with a unit in the Canadian Army.

The Korean War

Tommy finds it hard to get steady
work. He works in logging camps.
Another war starts in Korea. Tommy
joins the Army once again. Tommy
fights as only Tommy can. He wins
three medals. Tommy returns home
in 1953.

The
Korean War
starts in 1950
and ends in
1953.

Like many veterans, Tommy drinks to forget.

Life After the War

Tommy serves his country in two wars. The wars wound his body and his mind. Tommy suffers from a bad knee. The wars hurt Tommy's spirit even more. He has nightmares about the friends he lost in the wars. To forget, Tommy drinks too much.

Tommy lives at the Winnipeg Salvation Army hostel.

Life After the War

For many years, Tommy works at odd
jobs. Many white men look down
on Tommy because he is Indian.
The nightmares continue. Tommy
continues to drink. In the white world,
one of Canada's great heroes is a
forgotten man.

Tommy is honoured in Winnipeg.

Life After the War

Later in life, Tommy quits drinking. He grows closer to his children, now adults. White people start to hear the Tommy Prince story. Tommy always holds his head high. People honour this proud man who loves Canada.

These people pay their respects at Tommy Prince's grave.

A Hero Dies

Tommy dies in 1977. He is 62 years old. When he dies, two of his daughters are by his side. Five hundred people go to his funeral. People from all walks of life pay their respects. They remember a hero.

Tommy's monument in Winnipeg.

A Hero Dies

Chief Peguis dies 50 years before
Tommy is born. Tommy only
knows stories about his great-great-
grandfather. Today, statues of both
men stand across from each other.
You can see them together in a park
in Winnipeg.

Glossary

---

combat: active fighting, especially in a war.

Indian: Indigenous people in Canada who are not Inuit or Métis. The term First Nations has replaced the word Indian.

mission: a military task.

paratrooper: a soldier trained to land in combat areas by parachuting from planes.

reserve: land set aside by treaty for First Nations people.

veteran: a person who has served in the military forces.

Talking About the Book

What did you learn about Tommy Prince?

Do you think Tommy was a leader?
Why or why not?

In your opinion, why did the Army ask
Tommy to join the Devil's Brigade?

Describe Tommy's acts of courage in
Italy and France.

What challenges did Tommy face in his life?

Picture Credits

Front cover photos (center photo): © QMI Agency. **Contents page (top right):** © Manitoba Museum; **(bottom left):** Library and Archives Canada/Department of National Defence/PA-128264; **(bottom right):** © BattlefieldHistorian/BHC 000283. **Page 4:** © Government of Canada. Reproduced with the permission of the Minister of Public Works and Government Services Canada (2015). Source: Library and Archives Canada/Department of National Defence fonds/e010782857. **Page 6:** © Library and Archives Canada/e010956381. **Page 8:** © Library of Congress/ LC-USZ62-133499. **Page 10:** Glenbow Museum NA-2791-9. **Page 12:** © Curtis, Edward S., Library of Congress. **Page 14:** © Library and Archives Canada, Acc. No. 1977-64-11. **Page 16:** © Sgt. Elmer R. Bonter / Canada. Dept. of National Defence / Library and Archives Canada / PA-179718. **Page 18:** © Lieut. C.E. Nye / Canada. Dept. of National Defence / Library and Archives Canada / PA-128986. **Page 20:** © C.E. Nye / Canada. Dept. of National Defence / Library and Archives Canada / PA-183867. **Page 22:** © BattlefieldHistorian/BHC 000415. **Page 24:** © BattlefieldHistorian/BHC 000283. **Page 26:** © Library and Archives Canada/ Paul E. Tomelin/Department of National Defence. **Page 28:** © BattlefieldHistorian/ BHC 050073. **Page 30:** © Christopher J. Woods / Canada Dept. of National Defence / Library and Archives Canada / PA-142289. **Page 32:** © Glenbow Museum NA-5600-6507a. **Page 34:** © Library and Archives Canada/PA-114890. **Page 36:** Bigstock 2401552. **Page 38:** © QMI Agency. **Page 40:** Glenbow Museum PA-3820-1-8. **Page 42:** © Winnipeg Free Press. **Page 44:** © Manitoba Museum.